I0392770

Coloring Book

DREAM CATCHERS

First Edition

Distributed by : CreateSpace

ISBN-13: 978-1537196909

ISBN-10: 1537196901

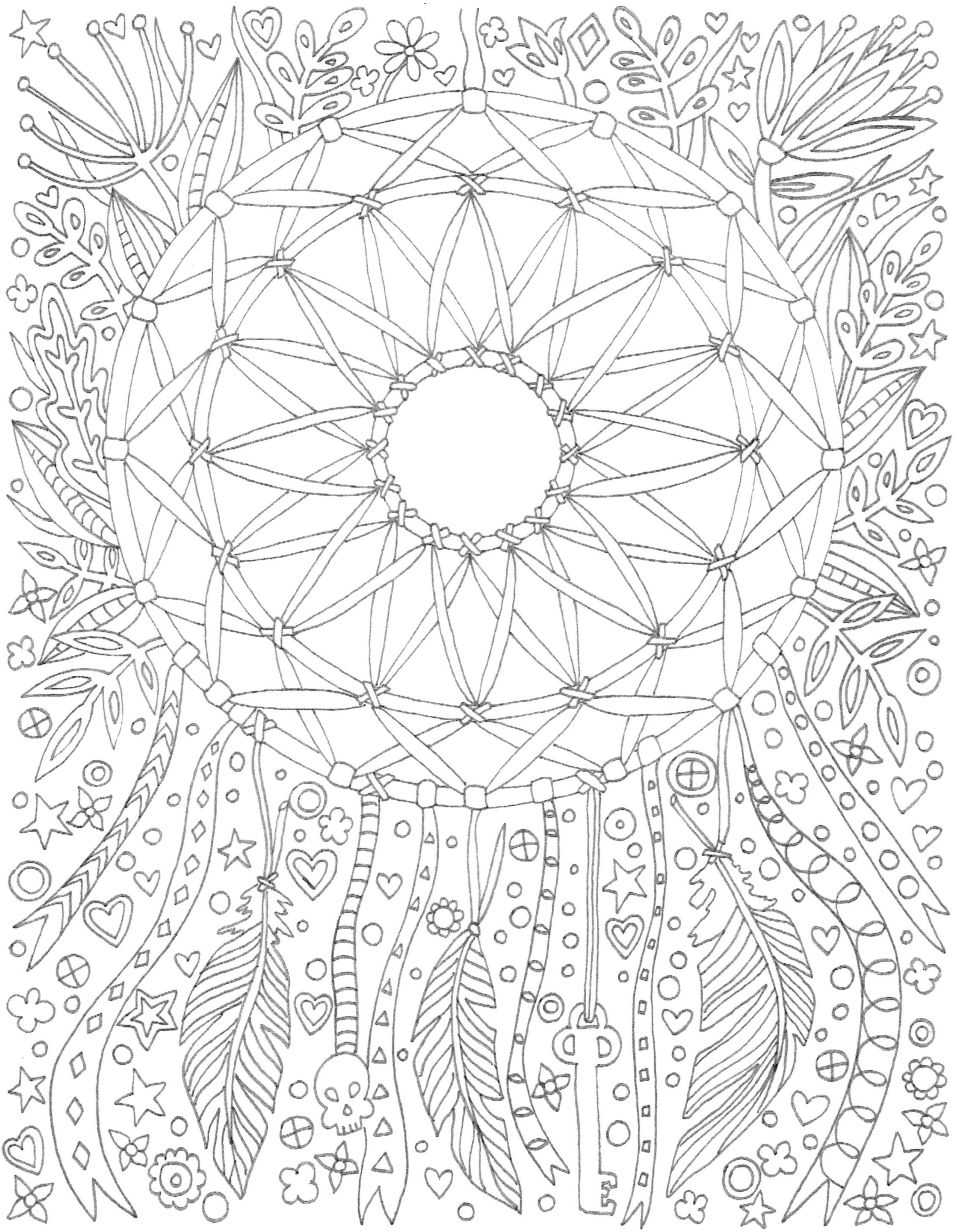

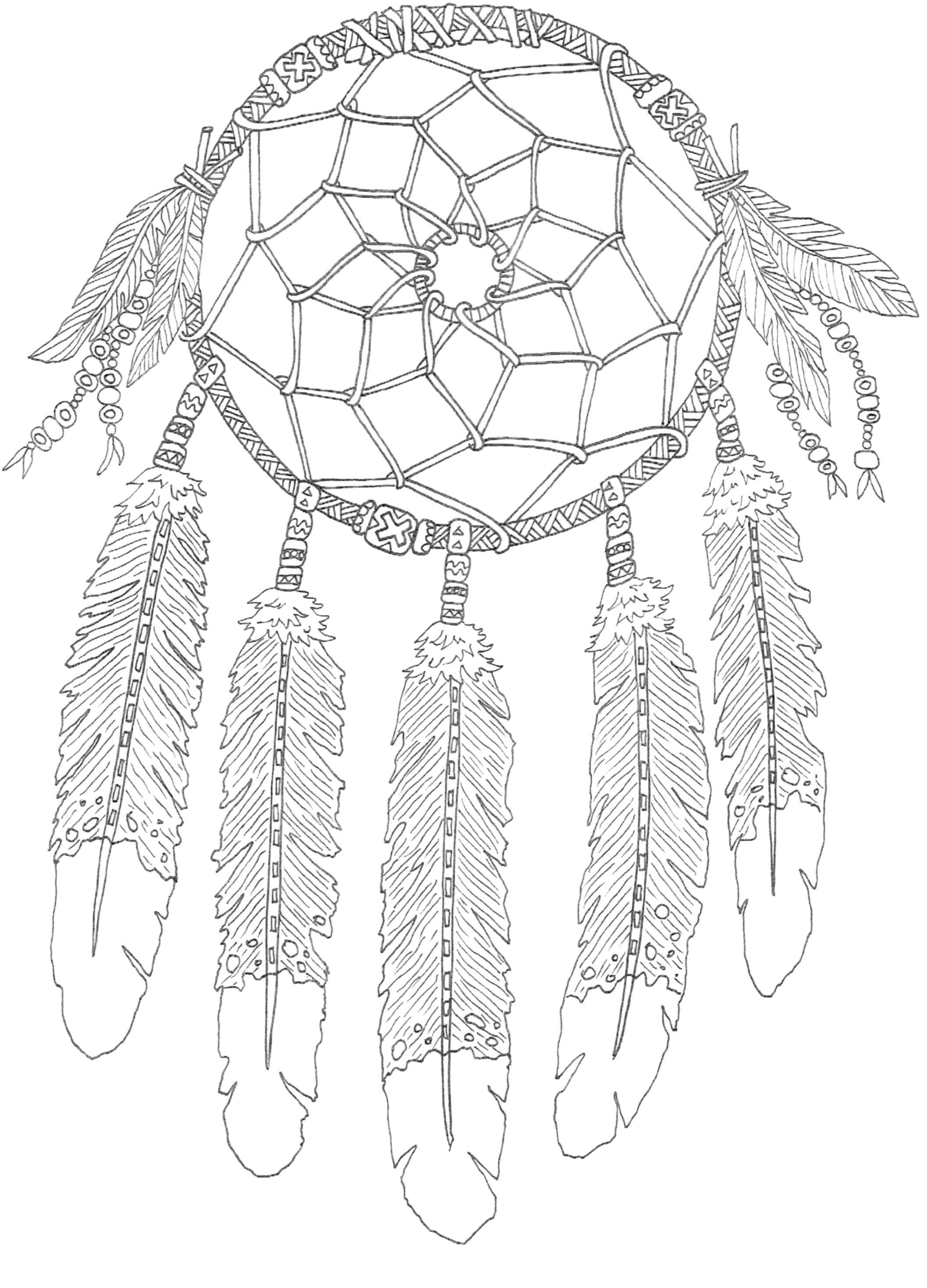

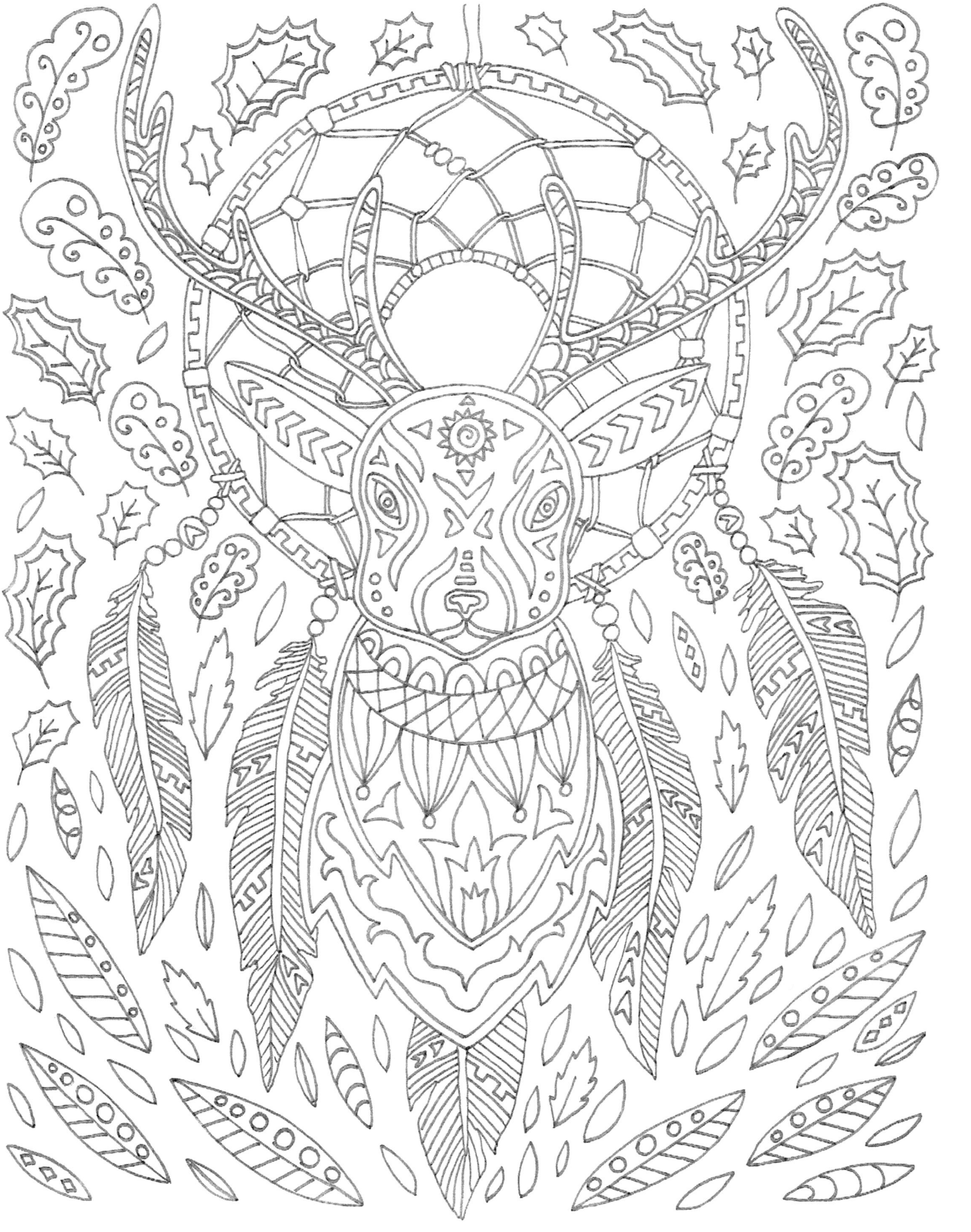

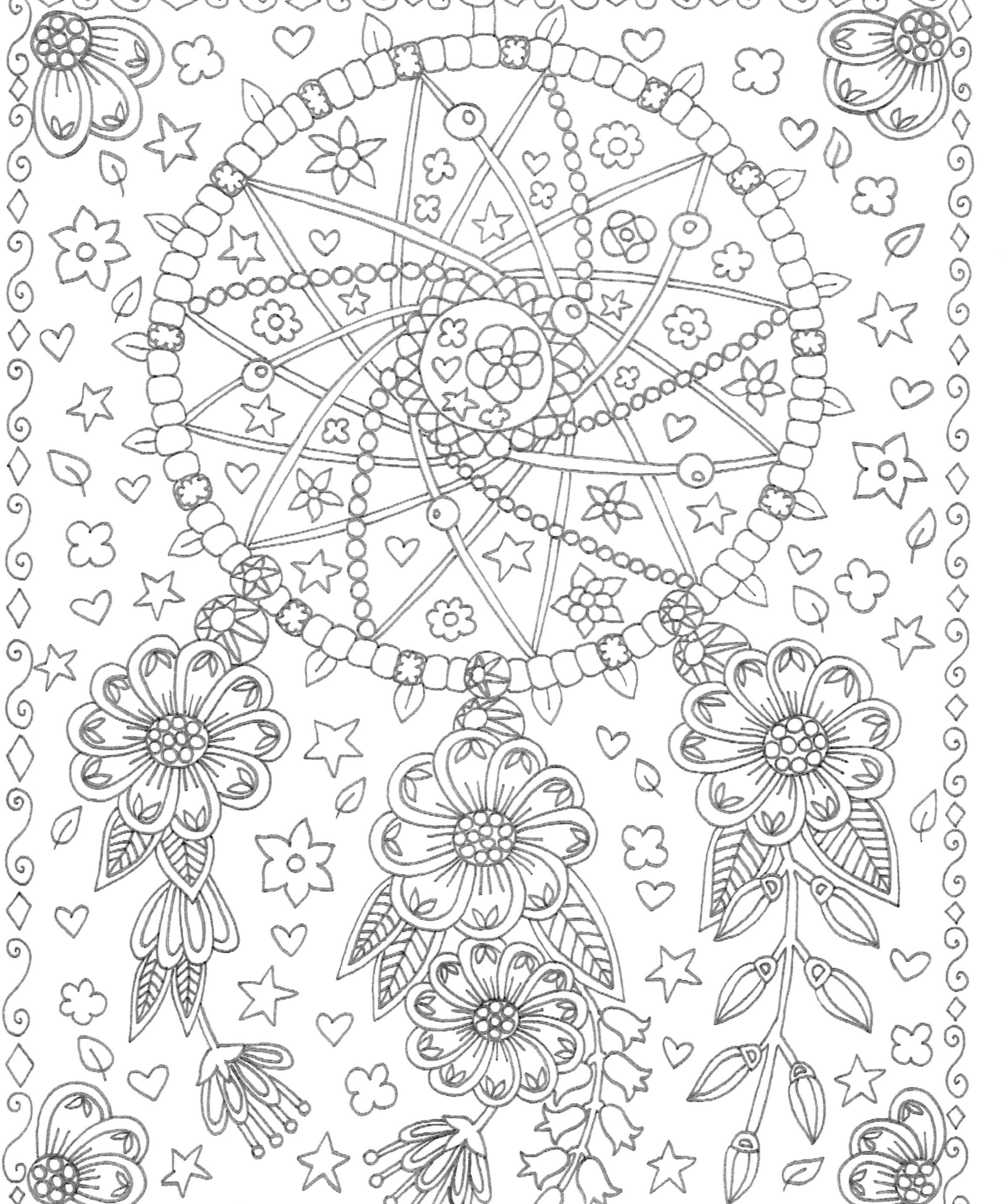

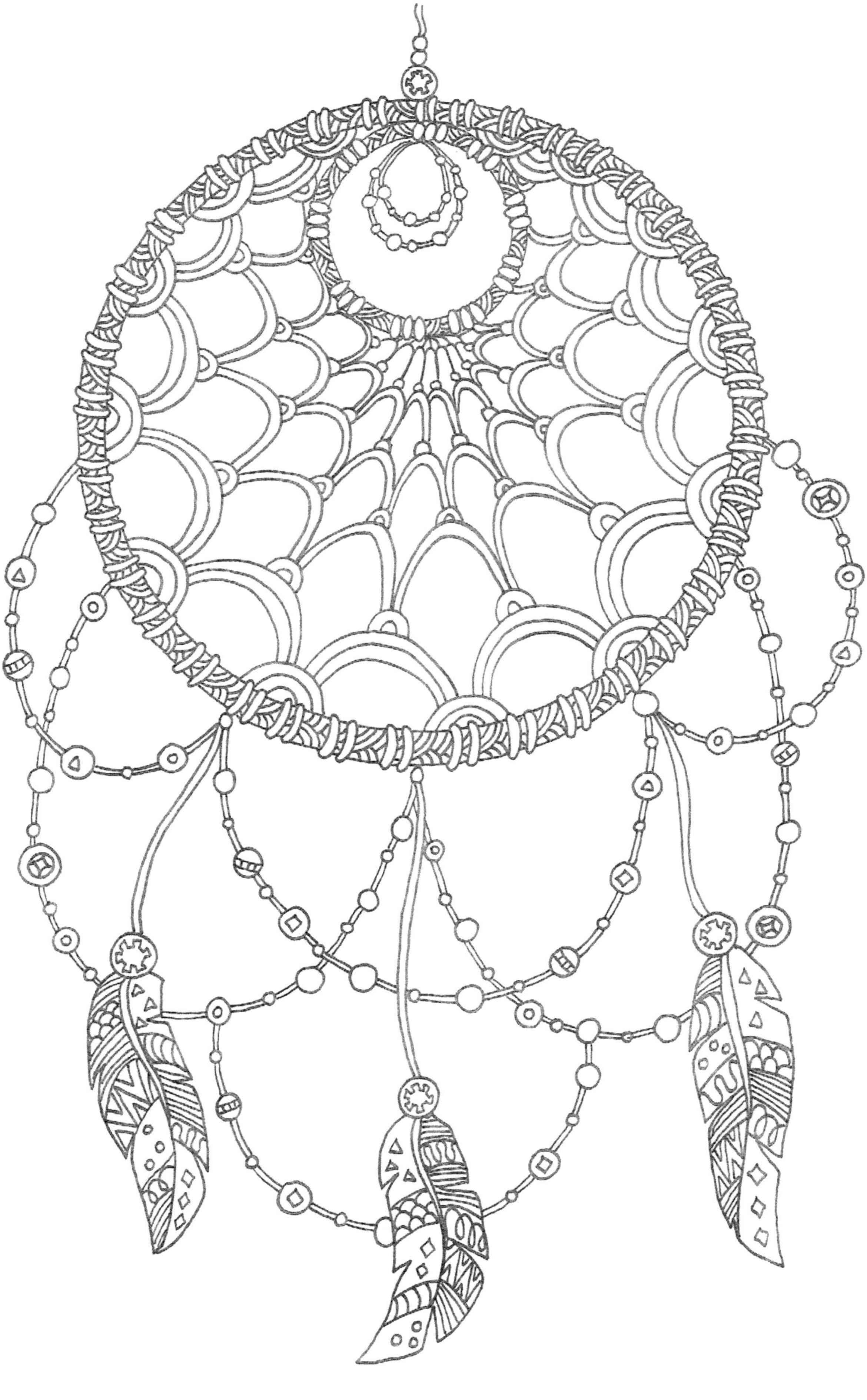

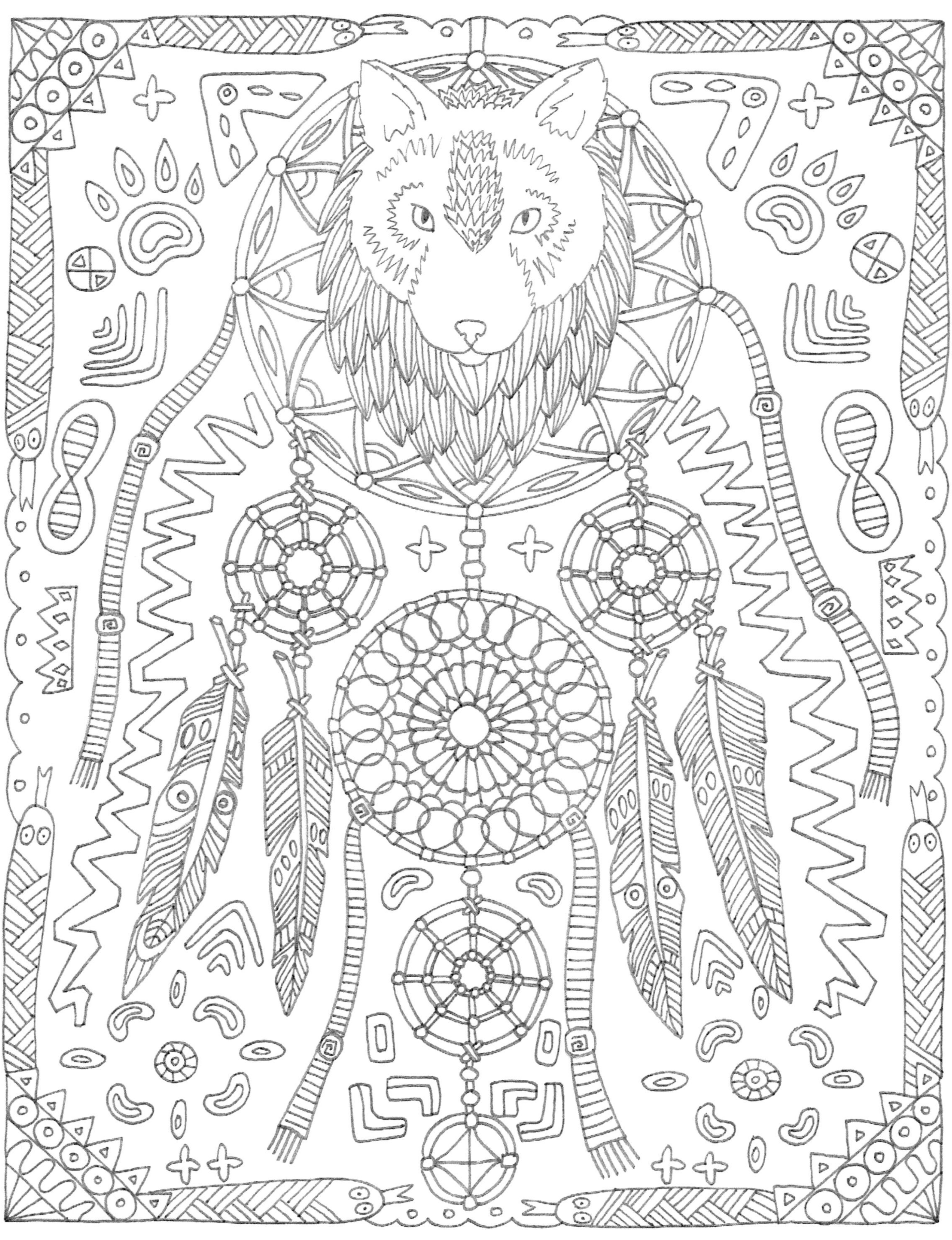

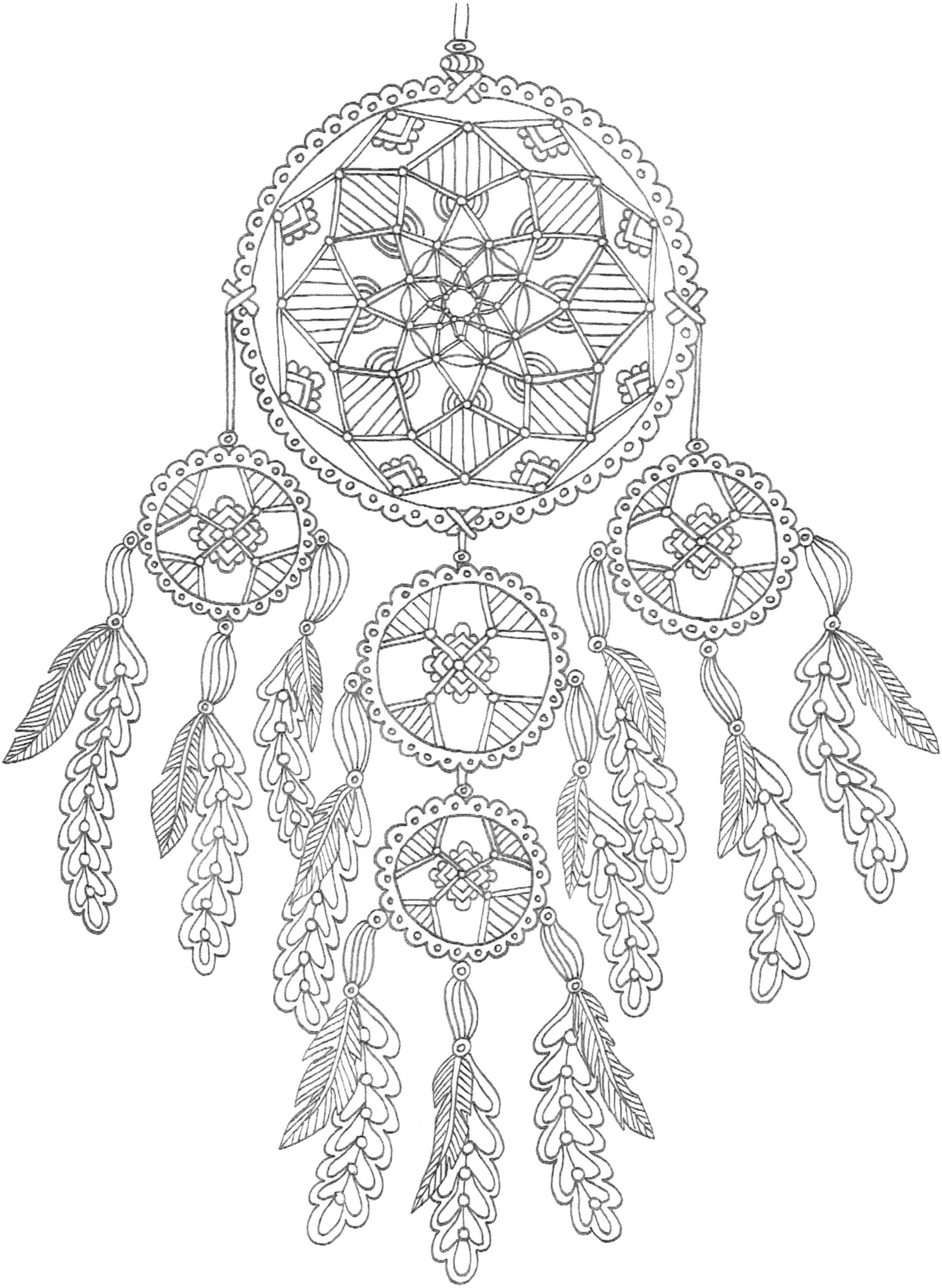

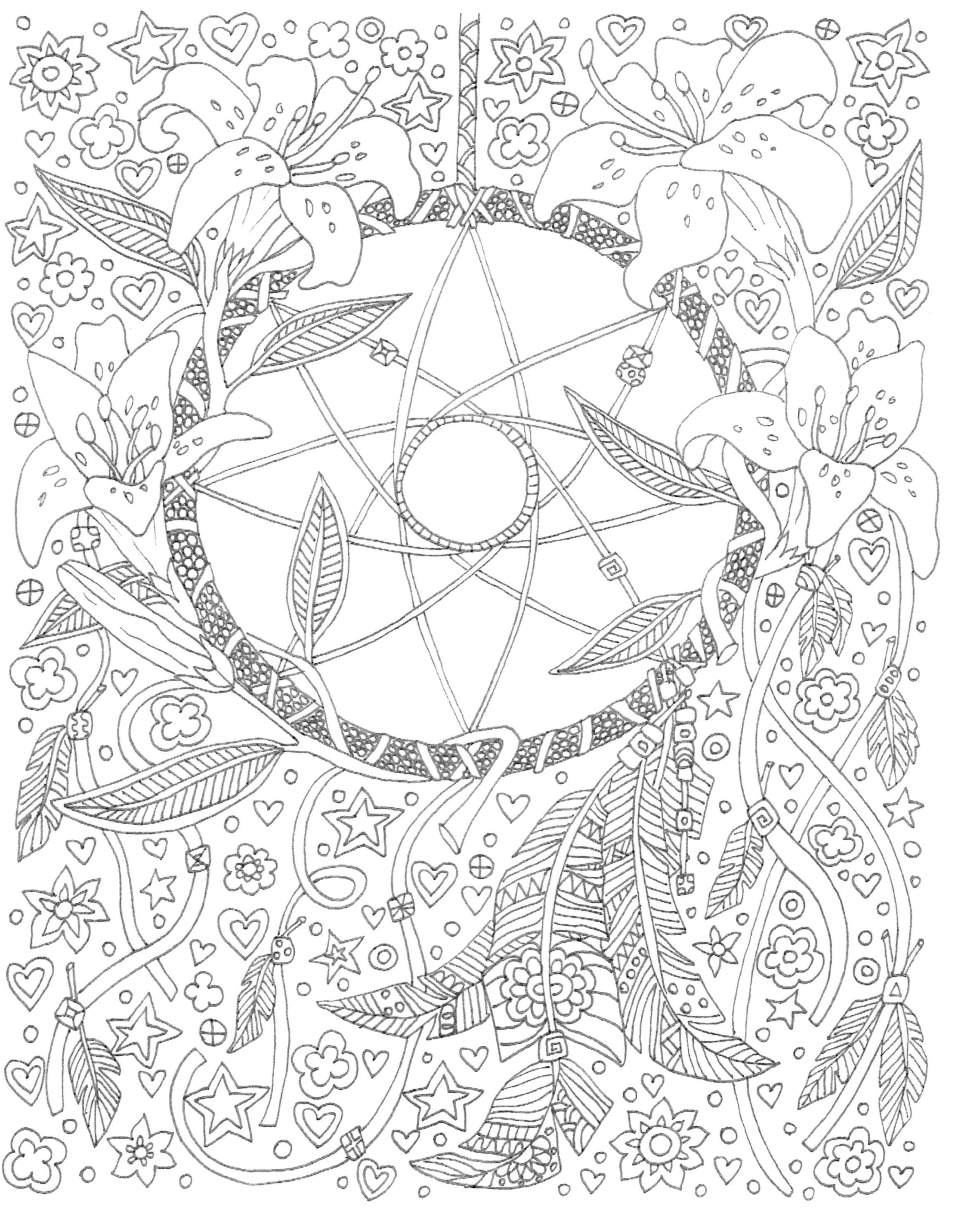

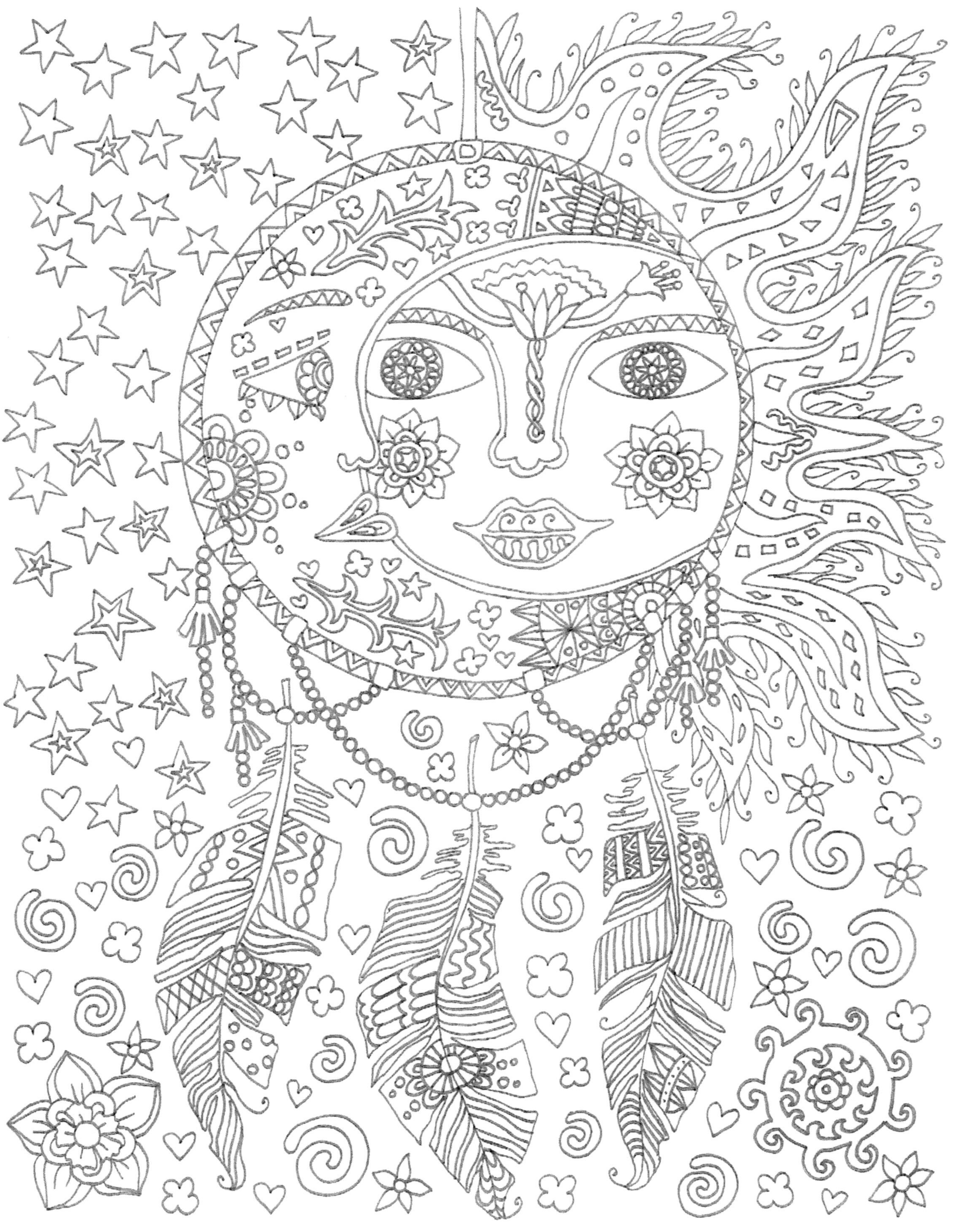

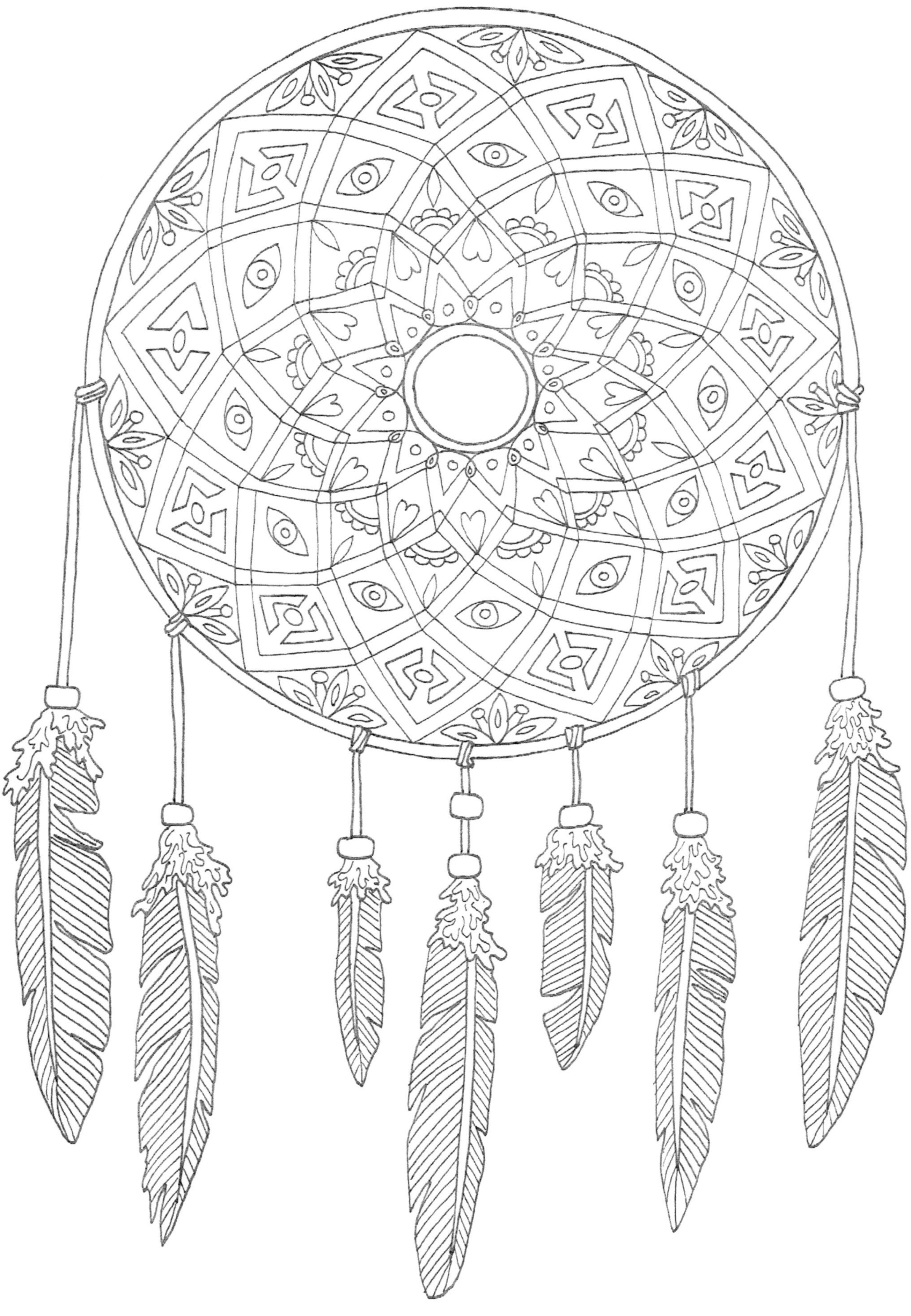

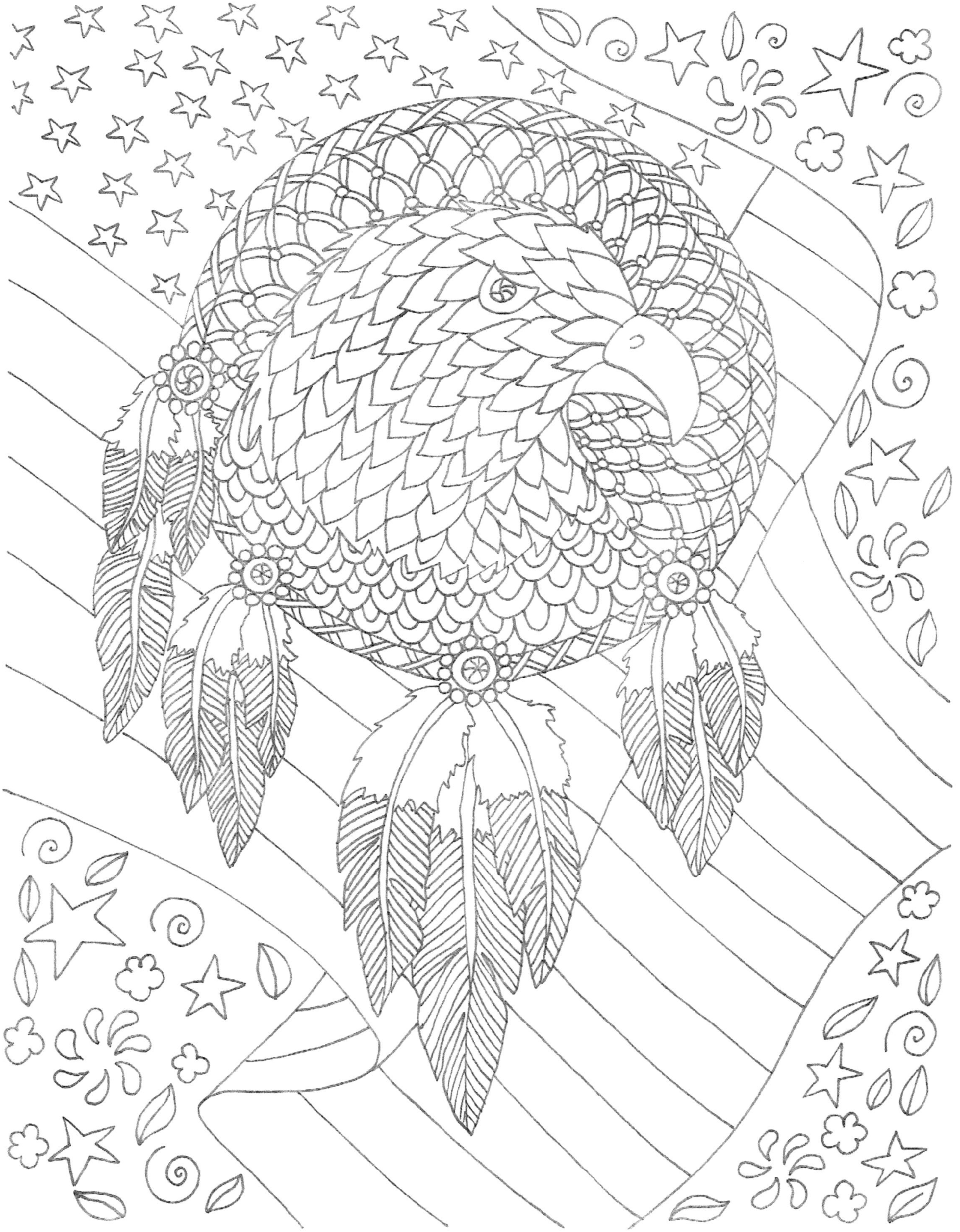

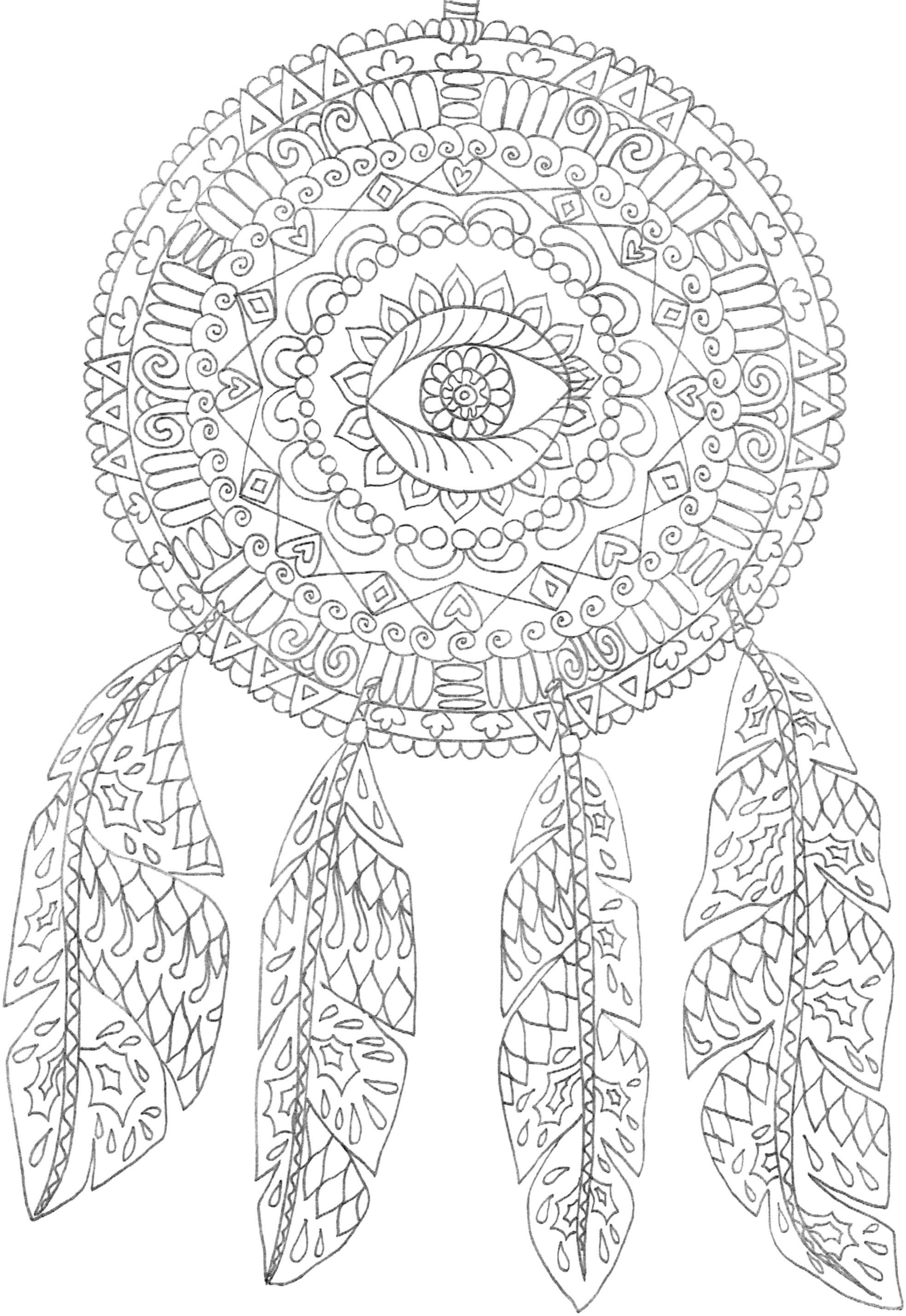

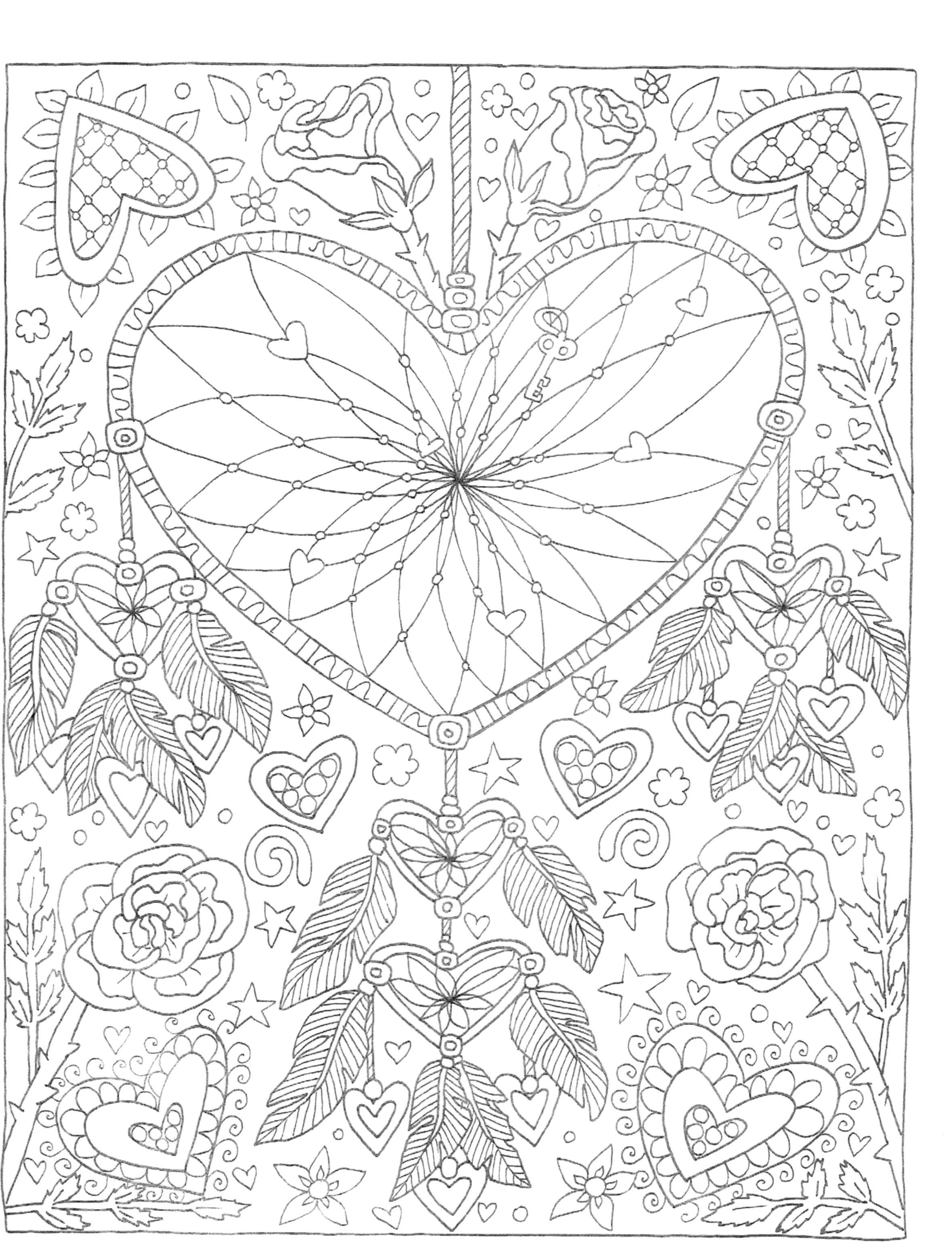

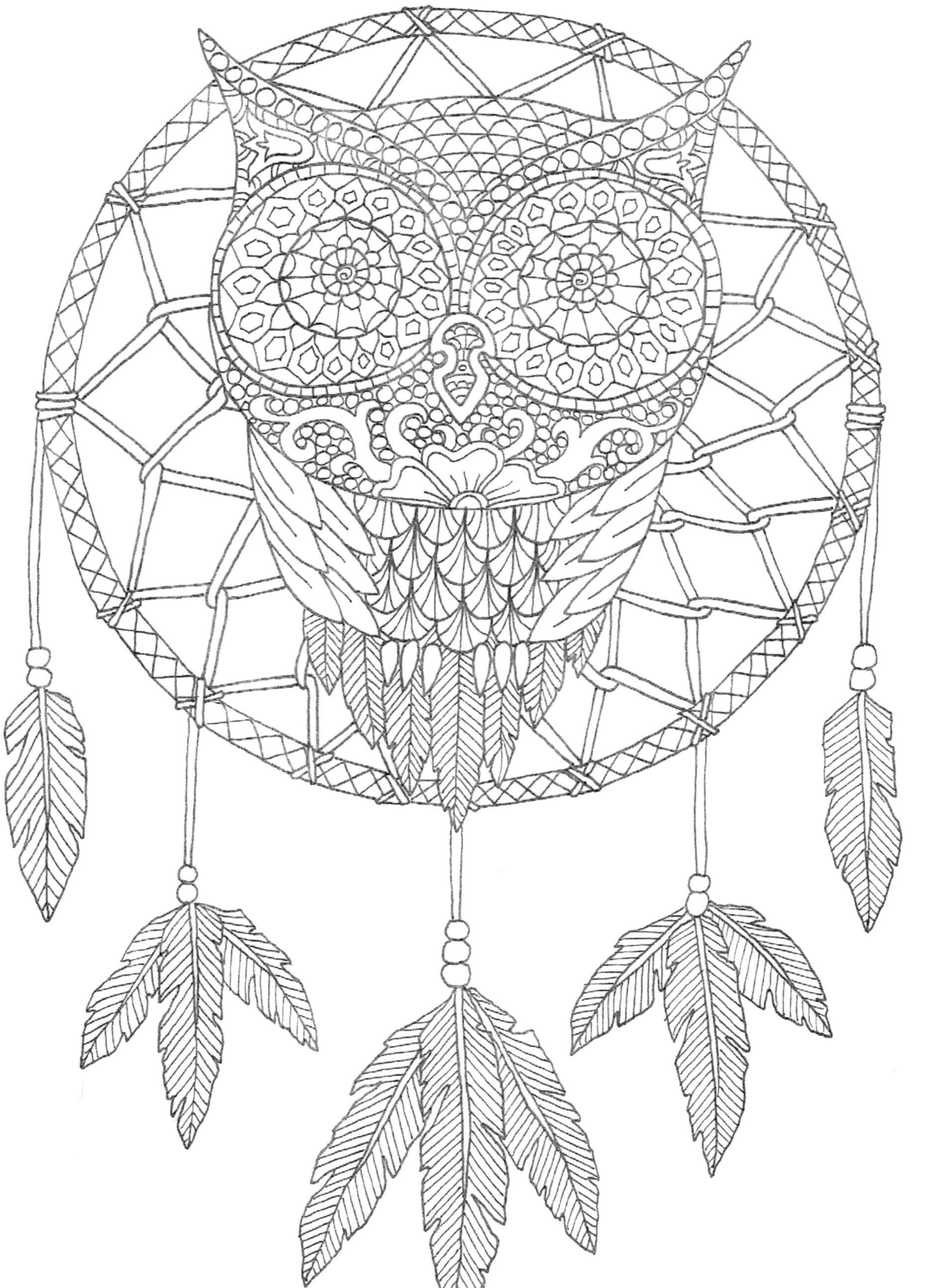

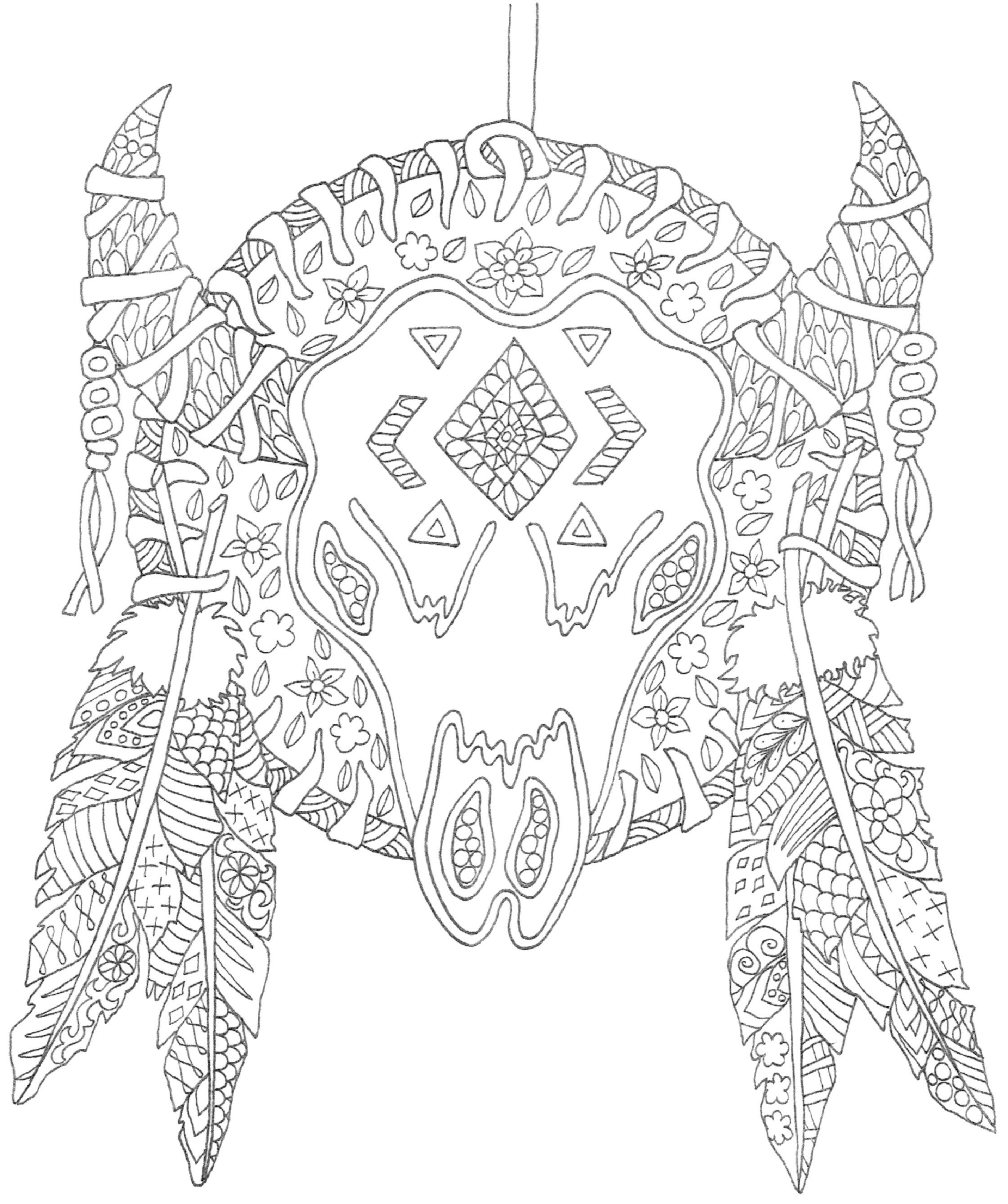

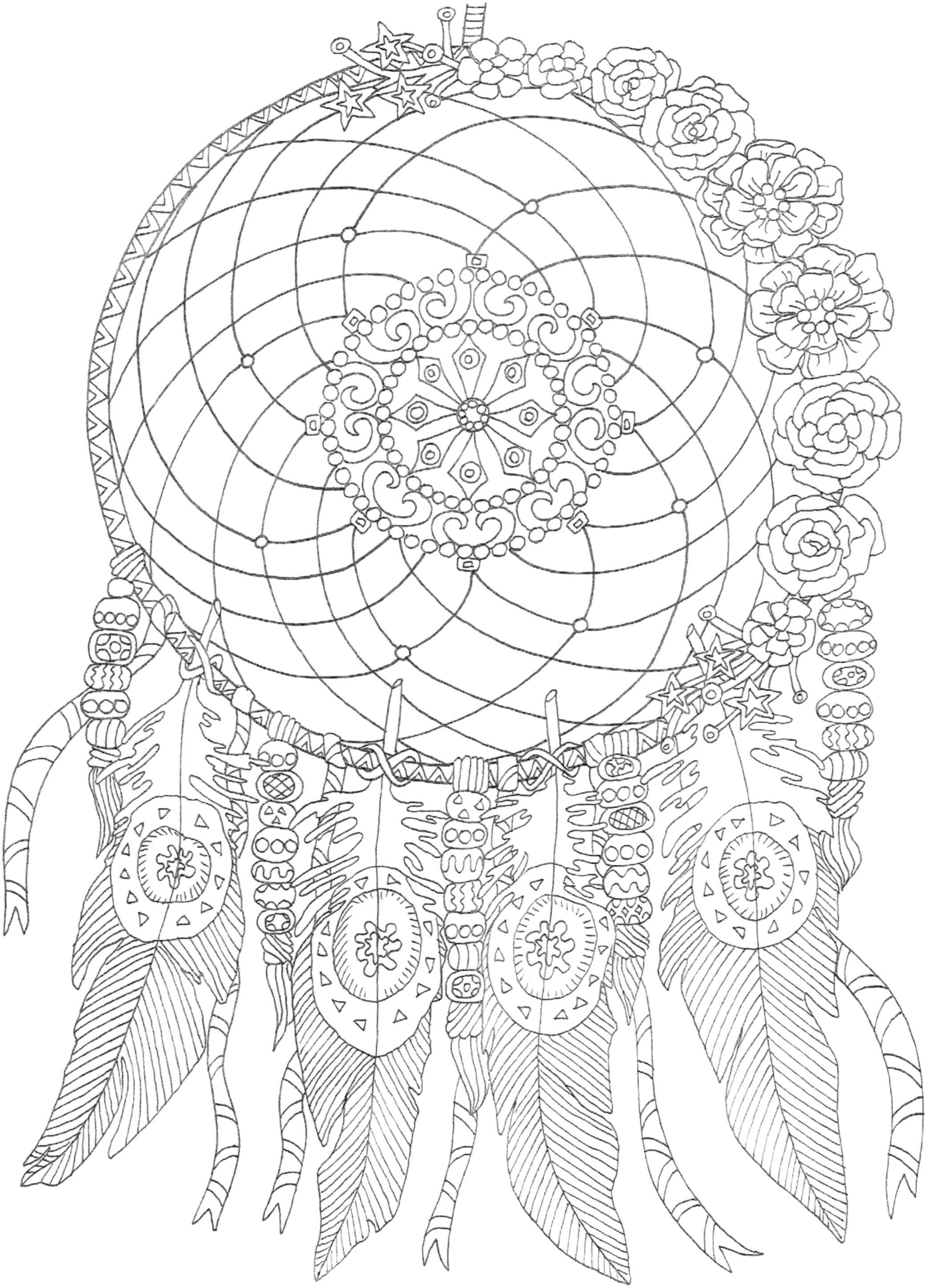

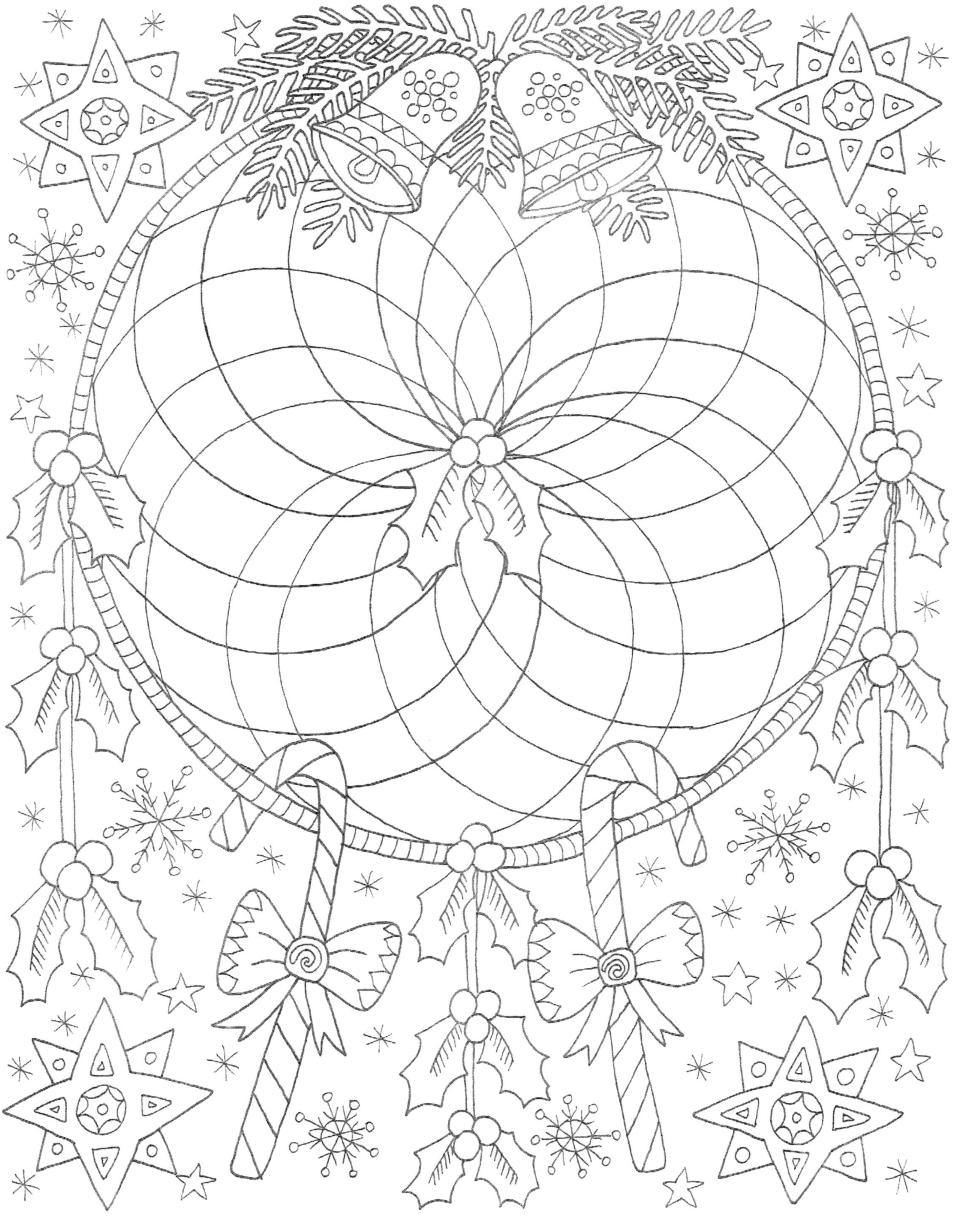

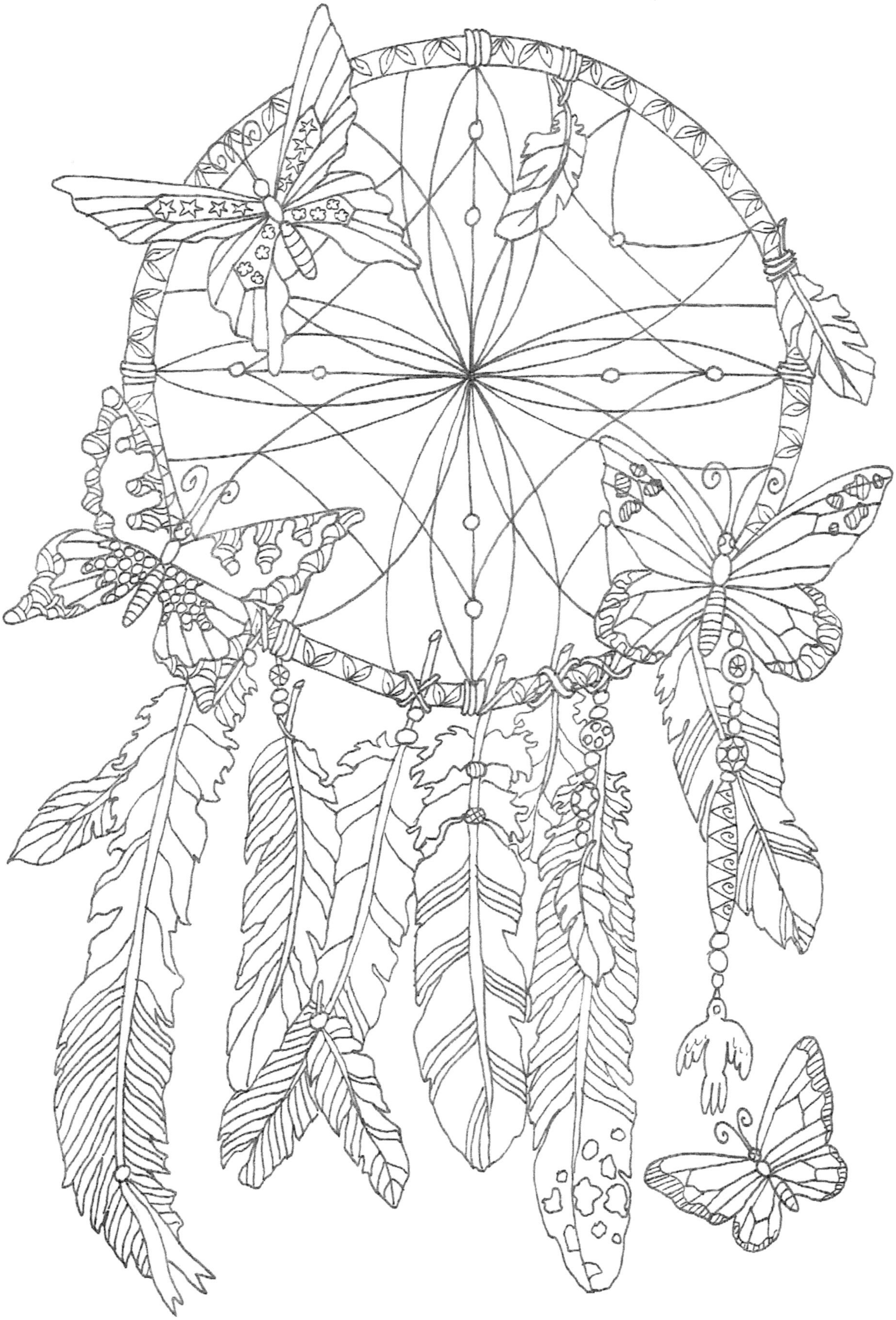

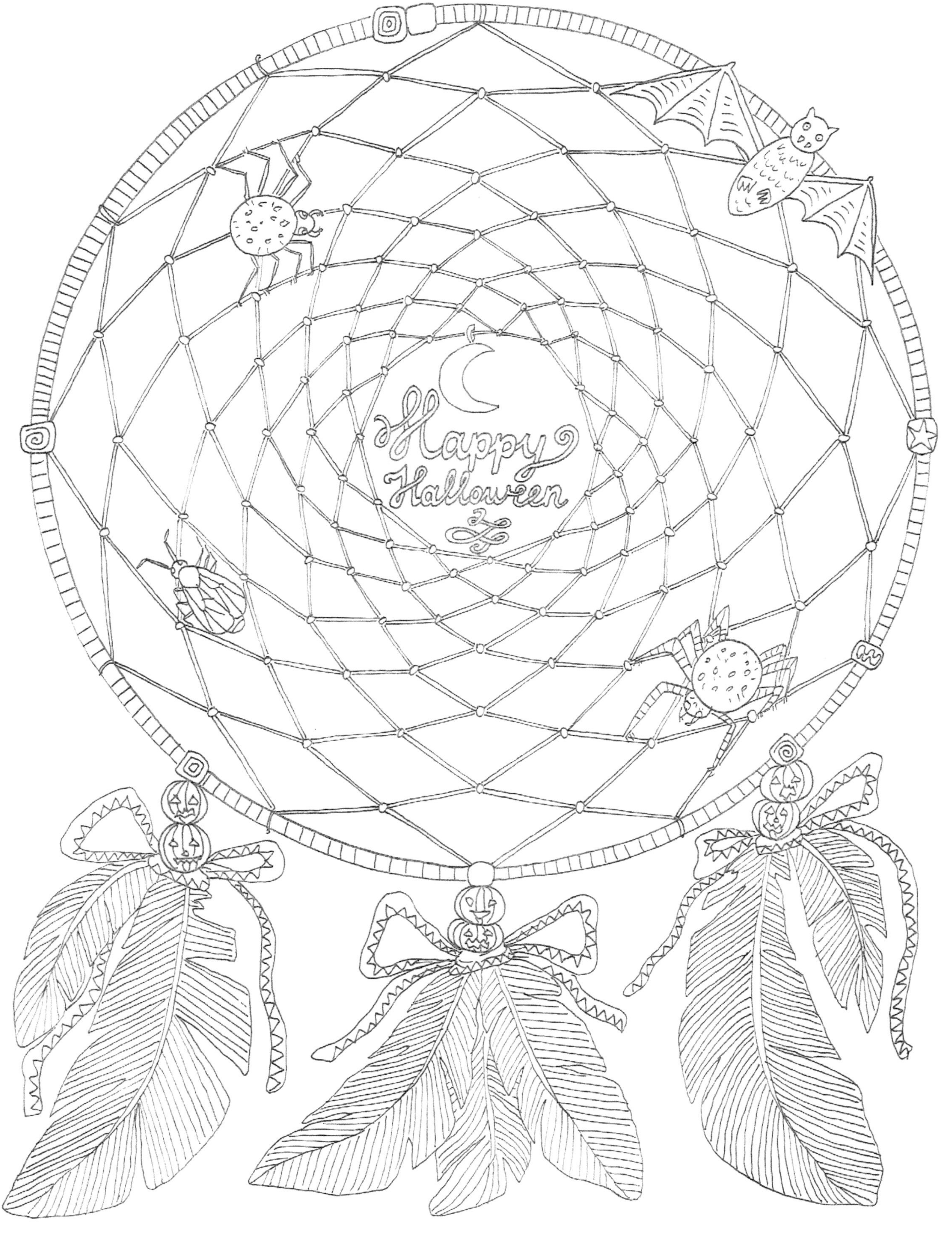
Happy Halloween

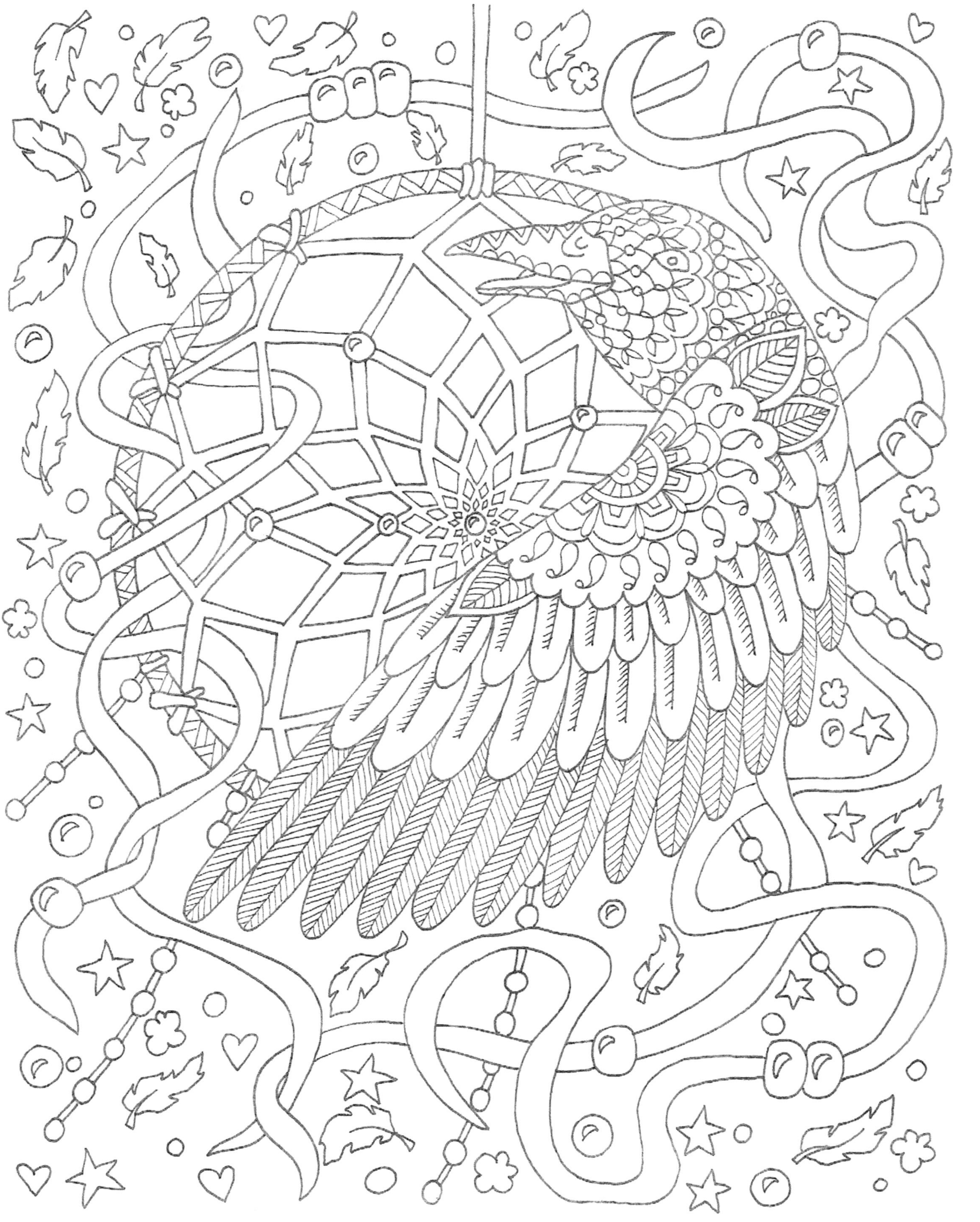

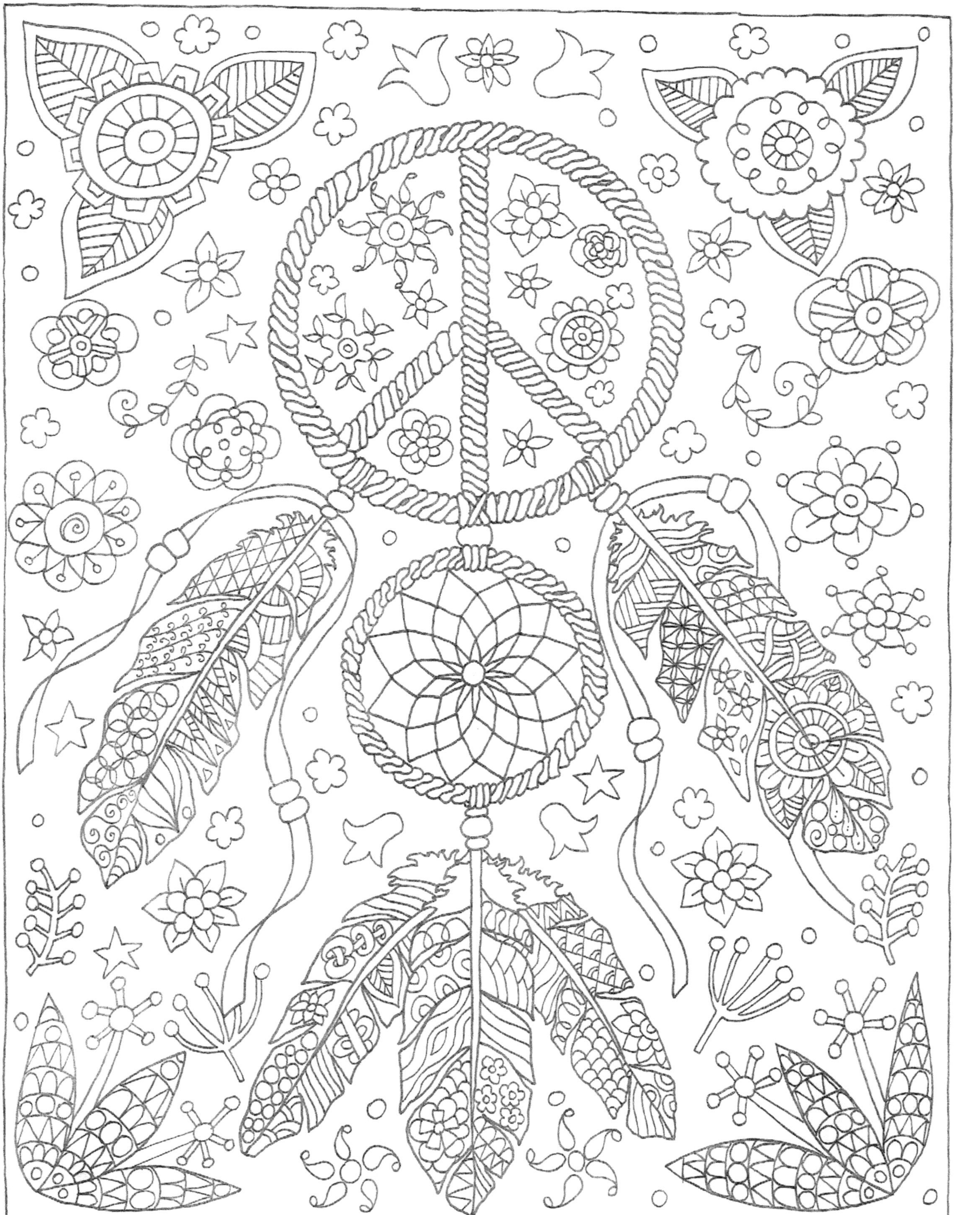

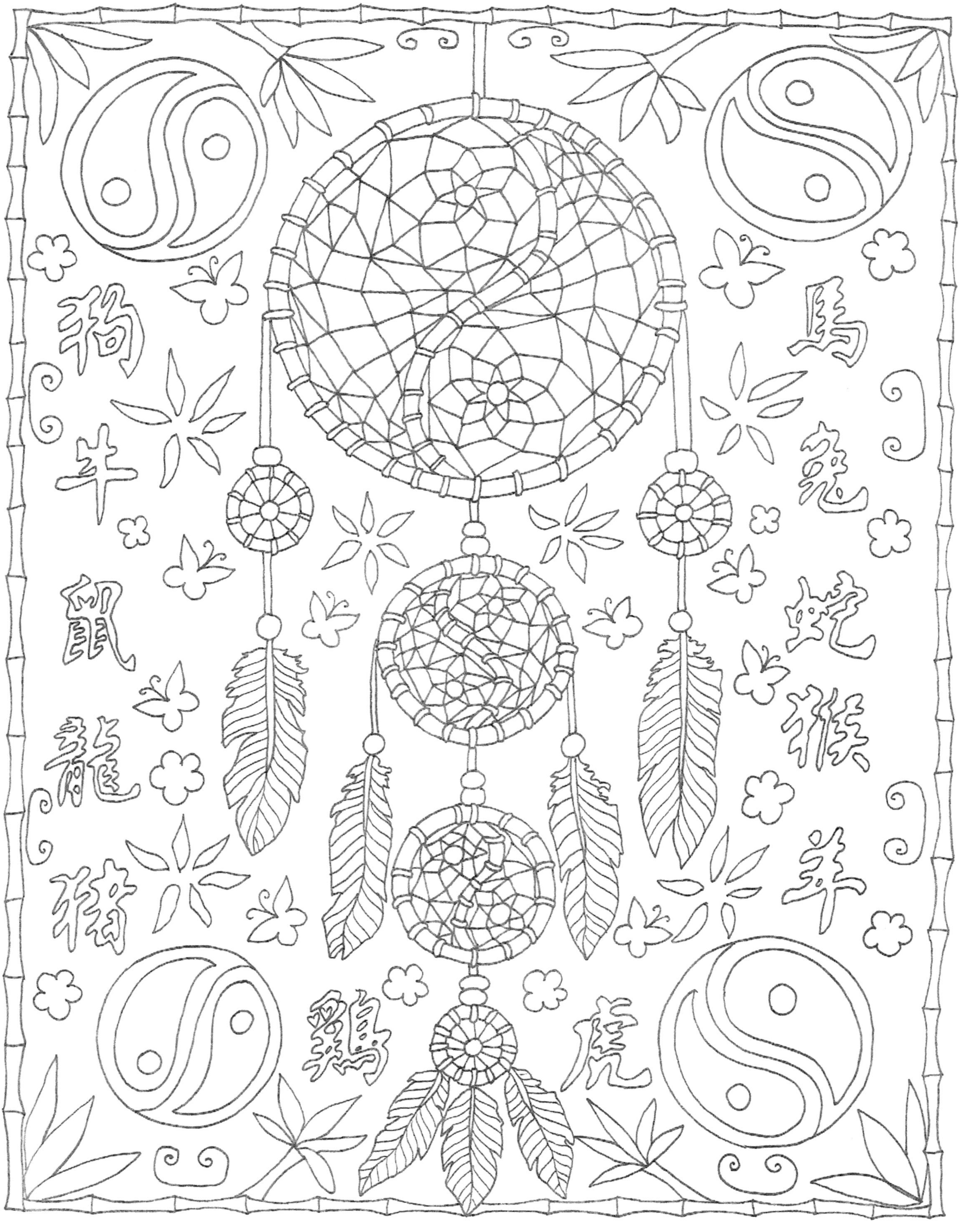

狗
牛
鼠
龍
猪
馬
兔
蛇
猴
羊
鷄
虎

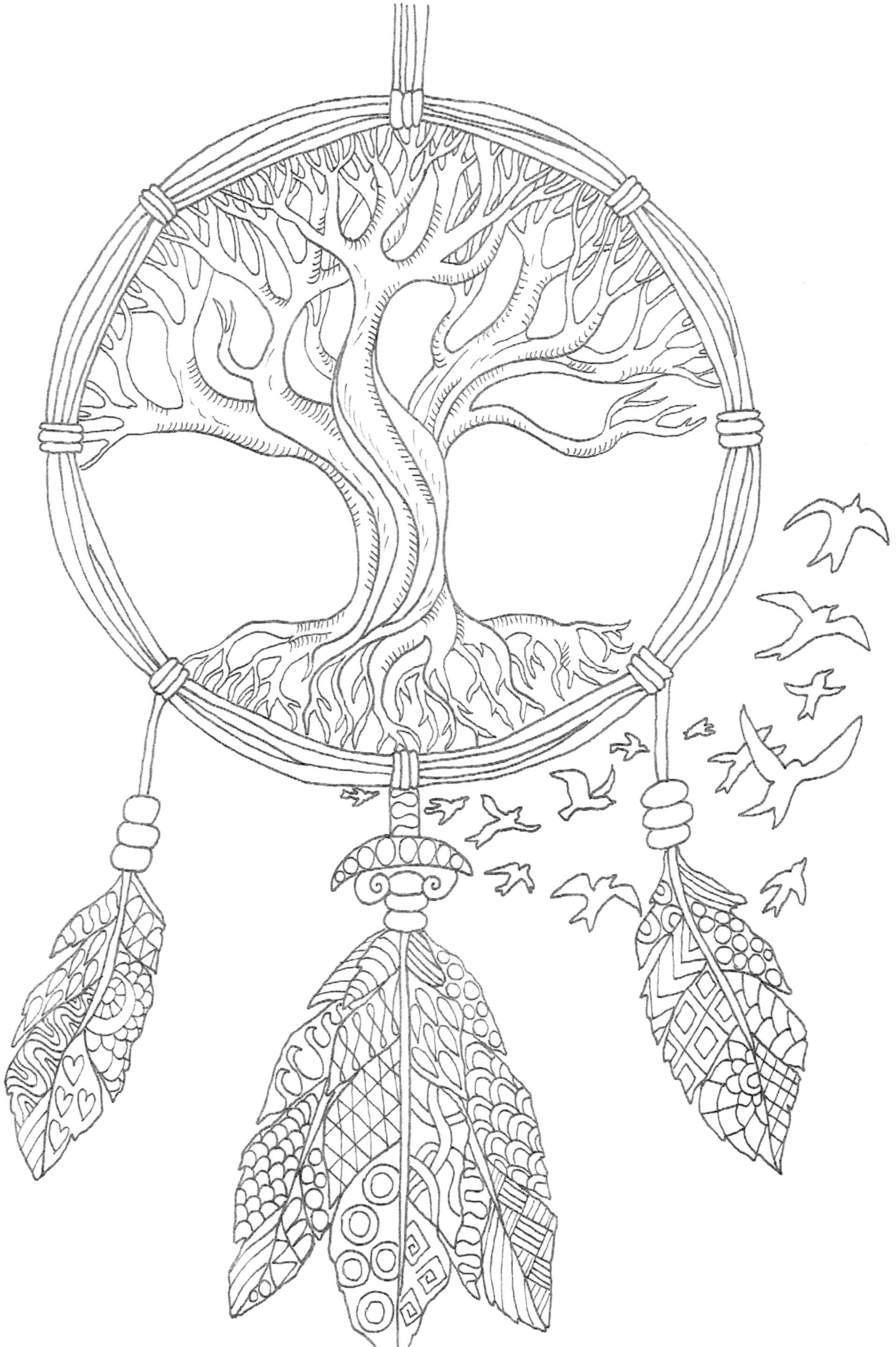

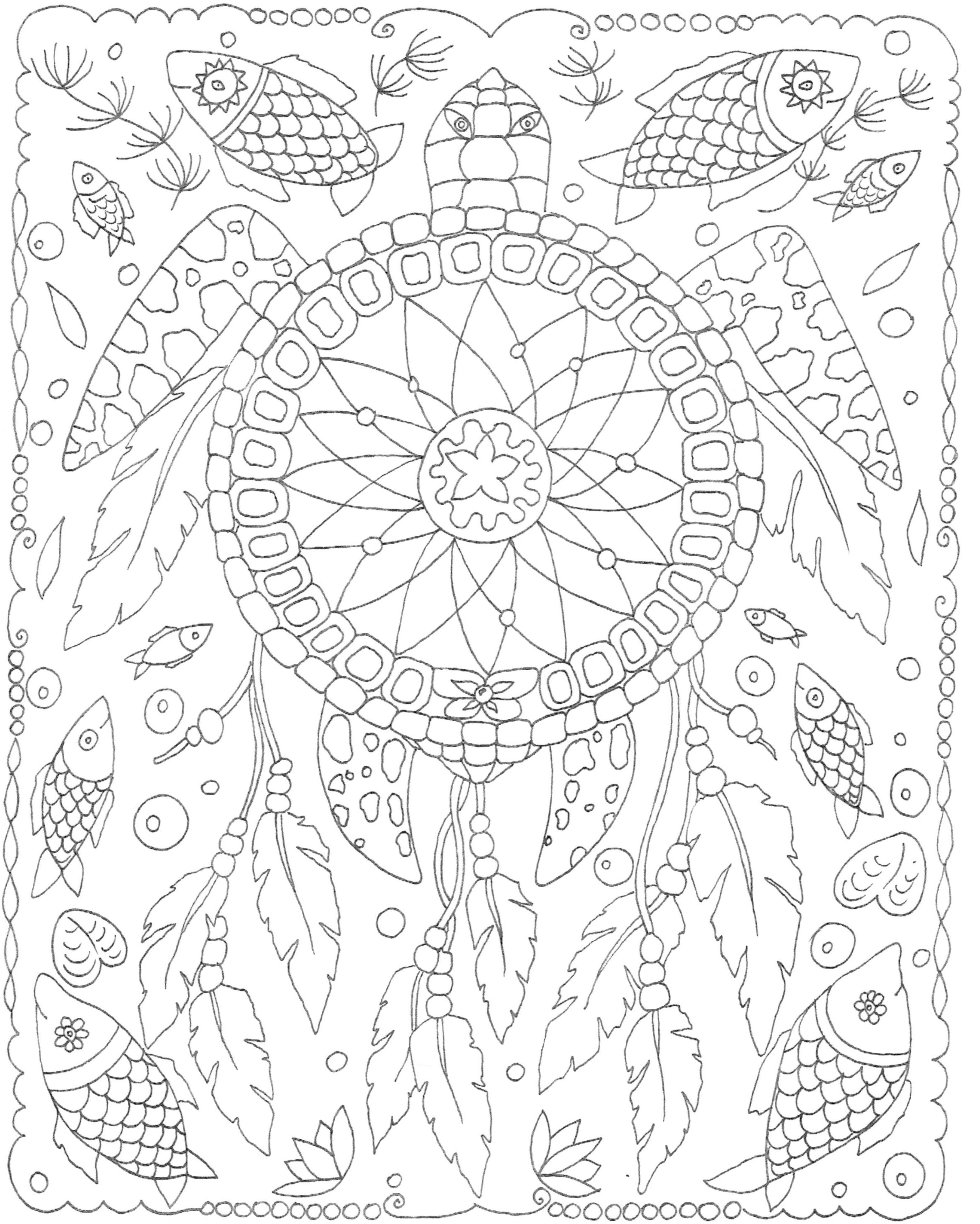

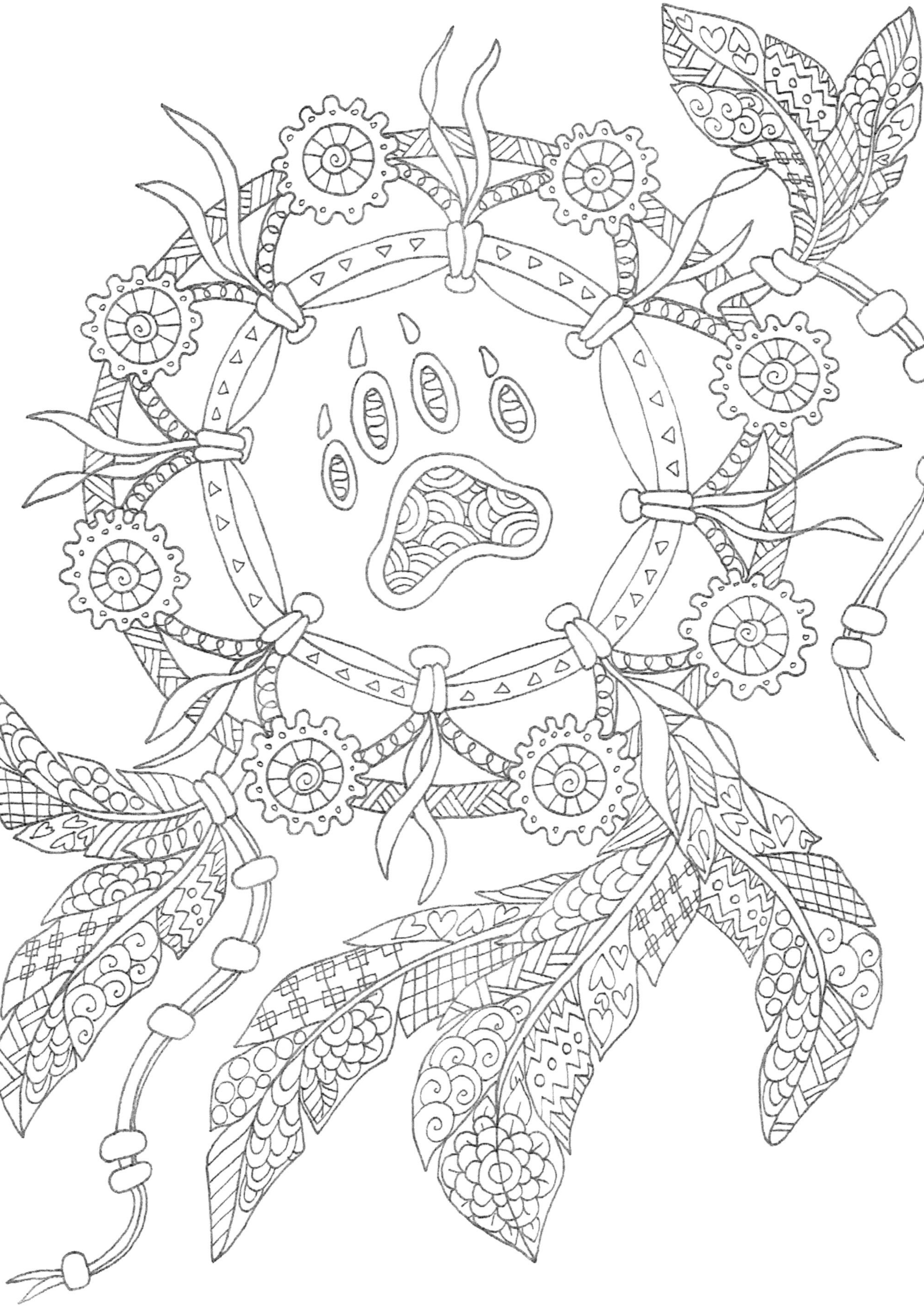

www.ingramcontent.com/pod-product-compliance
Lightning Source LLC
Chambersburg PA
CBHW080557190526
45169CB00007B/2803
* 9 7 8 1 5 3 7 1 9 6 9 0 9 *